THROUGH GEORGIA'S EYES

Rachel Rodríguez

illustrated by

Julie Paschkis

Henry Holt and Company

New York

AUTHOR'S NOTE

In telling the story of Georgia O'Keeffe's life, I read all I could about her and tried to discover the details of her life that would enchant young readers as they did me. I've told this story in homage to her art, her words, and her singular perspective as a woman artist in her time.

ILLUSTRATOR'S NOTE

In this book I refer to photographs of Georgia O'Keeffe and to paintings by her. I wanted to quote specific paintings and photographs, but I didn't want to try to re-create her paintings, so I translated the images into cut-paper collages. The simplicity of this medium reflects her modern aesthetic. To create each collage, I painted sheets of paper in gradating color using acrylic paint and then cut out the shapes and glued them down in layers.

BIBLIOGRAPHY

Castro, Jan Garden. *The Art and Life of Georgia O'Keeffe*. New York: Crown, 1985.

Lisle, Laurie. *Portrait of an Artist: A Biography of Georgia O'Keeffe*. New York: Washington Square Press, 1997.

O'Keeffe, Georgia. *Georgia O'Keeffe*. A Studio Book. New York: Viking Press, 1976.

————. *Some Memories of Drawing*. Albuquerque: University of New Mexico Press, 1988.

Turner, Elizabeth Hutton. *Georgia O'Keeffe: The Poetry of Things*. New Haven: Yale University Press, 1999.

Henry Holt and Company, LLC, *Publishers since 1866*
175 Fifth Avenue, New York, New York 10010
www.henryholtchildrensbooks.com

Henry Holt® is a registered trademark of Henry Holt and Company, LLC.

Library of Congress Cataloging-in-Publication Data
Rodríguez, Rachel.
Through Georgia's eyes / Rachel Rodríguez ; illustrated by Julie Paschkis.—1st ed.
p.   cm.
ISBN-13: 978-0-8050-7740-7
ISBN-10: 0-8050-7740-5
1. O'Keeffe, Georgia, 1887–1986—Juvenile literature. 2. Painters—United States—
Biography—Juvenile literature. 3. Picture books for children. I. Paschkis, Julie, ill. II. Title.
ND237.O5R63 2006   759.13—dc22   2005012479

First Edition—2006 / Designed by Donna Mark / Printed in the United States of America on acid-free paper. ∞
10 9 8 7 6 5 4 3 2 1

To Georgia, for showing me the path, and Mom,
for cheering my every step along it —R. R.

For Julan Chu —J. P.

SUN PRAIRIE, WISCONSIN, 1887

Georgia's first memory:

She will always remember these colors and the brightness
of light—light all around.

Soon Georgia runs and plays games with her brothers and
sisters. Her father gives her sweets and plays Irish tunes.
Her mother reads stories and cares for the younger children.
Everyone works hard on the farm.

Georgia roams the prairie. The trees and land keep her company. Pencil and sketch pad comfort her. She discovers she likes to be alone.

Seasons melt into seasons on her family's farm. Georgia struggles to show on paper what she sees.

At twelve, she takes painting lessons. She tells her friend,
"I am going to be an artist." But in 1899 only boys
become artists. A girl wishing to be one is scandalous.

Georgia sees life differently. She paints and paints. Hours pass without notice. She wonders if she can achieve her dream.

She walks around a lake and hikes into the woods.
Everywhere she looks, shapes hum and sing to her.

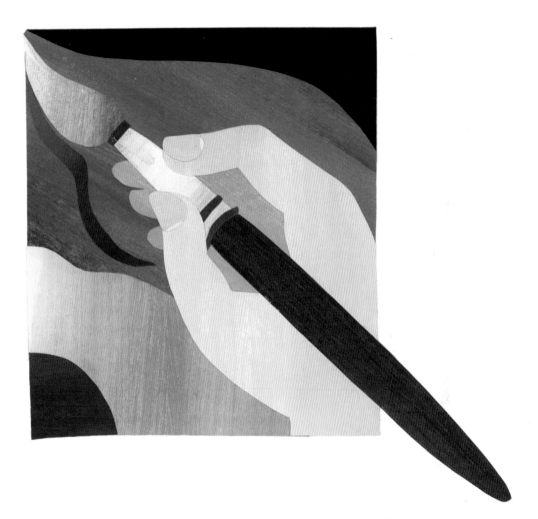

At art school, brushes and canvas become her language. Paint speaks for her. Watercolor and oil are her words.

For a time, Georgia lives in the city. She walks through canyons of concrete. She misses the outdoor world. The sun steals a bite from a skyscraper. The Faraway place—open sky and land—calls her.

The wideness and wonder of the world amaze Georgia. She wants to share this magic with others.

Flowers delight her. She paints them as giants. People stop to stare. Georgia's flowers make them feel like tiny butterflies, flitting through the universe of her garden.

She moves to Ghost Ranch in New Mexico. Red hills, cliffs, silence, and the Faraway surround her.

In the desert, she discovers extraordinary things— skulls. The bones don't frighten Georgia. To her, they are alive and strong. Their beauty astounds her.

Georgia expresses feelings in her
own way. Words work. But for
her, the color blue says it better.
Or red. Or a seashell.
A pale bone.
Sunset.

The trees and hills whisper their secrets. They are friends, always there for her.

A canyon calls her. From the bottom at dusk she sees a long line of cows above, black lace against a dusky sky.

She hikes at dawn. She climbs a ridge.
The land enchants her.

A range of hills is a mile of elephants
with white sand at their feet.

Sometimes her Chow Chow tags along.

He hops around rocks and chases antelope.

They float ahead of her yelping dog.

Georgia follows them. She breathes in the dawn.
A sea of sage covers the plain before a mountain,
like waves lapping against a shore.

Sometimes she climbs a ladder to her roof.
The moon rises above.

Beneath a giant canvas of inky night and
silvery stars, Georgia dreams.

Even now, Georgia can show you the world as she sees it.

Open your eyes . . .

. . . and walk along.

See the colors? Hear the shapes singing?

No need to hurry.
Lean in . . . look closer.
Closer still.
There . . . the wideness
and wonder of the world.

Georgia Totto O'Keeffe was born in Sun Prairie, Wisconsin, on November 15, 1887, at her parents' farmhouse. She had an older brother, a younger brother, and four younger sisters.

O'Keeffe was born at a time when women were not allowed to vote. Women artists were unheard of, and even considered freakish. Her parents wanted her to be an art teacher. Still, she pursued an art education. She attended the Art Institute of Chicago and the Art Students League in New York City. O'Keeffe taught at public schools in Texas and at the University of Virginia. In her free time, she did her own painting, keeping her efforts private from the other teachers. She followed her art and her distinct voice, and held fast to her dream of earning a living as an artist.

In New York, photographer Alfred Stieglitz first showed her work in his gallery. The exhibit piqued art lovers' curiosity. More and more people became loyal fans of O'Keeffe's work. She became friends with Stieglitz, who encouraged her painting. Eventually, they married. At age thirty, she had her first solo gallery exhibit, and she soon sold her first painting, which showed a train moving through the twilight. She made frequent trips to New Mexico, a place of vast spaces and arid beauty that inspired her work. Eventually, she left Manhattan and moved to New Mexico for good.

Although she died at the age of ninety-eight on March 6, 1986, O'Keeffe's popularity continues to grow. Museums around the world, including the Georgia O'Keeffe Museum in Santa Fe, New Mexico, still show her work. O'Keeffe's bold, creative spirit and determination to live as an artist made a lasting contribution to the art world. To this day, her work encourages new generations of artists to see the world through their own eyes and to share that vision with others.